Bishop Kallistos ~~

*All booklets are published
thanks to the generosity of the supporters
of the Catholic Truth Society*

Contents

All rights reserved. First published 2014 by The Incorporated Catholic Truth Society, 40-46 Harleyford Road London SE11 5AY Tel: 020 7640 0042 Fax: 020 7640 0046. © 2014 The Incorporated Catholic Truth Society.

ISBN 978 1 86082 893 5

What Is the Jesus Prayer?

"Lord, teach us to pray", the apostles said to Jesus (*Lk* 11:1). It is a request that all of us make to God. How are we to enter into the mystery of living prayer? How can we advance from prayer repeated by our lips - from prayer as an external act - to prayer that is part of our inner being, a true union of our mind and heart with the Holy Trinity? How can we make prayer not merely something that we *do*, but something that we *are*? For that is what the world needs: not persons who *say* prayers from time to time, but persons who *are* prayer all the time.

When I was about twelve years old, I heard a story in a sermon, which I have never forgotten. It is, I believe, a story recounted by the Curé d'Ars, but the preacher did not mention his name. Once there was an old man who spent several hours each day in church. "What are you doing there?" his friends enquired. "I'm praying," he replied. "Praying!" they exclaimed. "There must be a great many things that you want to ask from God." With some indignation the old man responded, "I'm not asking God for anything." "What are you doing, then?" they said. And the old man replied, "I just sit and look at God, and God sits and looks at me."

At the age of twelve, I thought that an admirable description of prayer, and I still think so today. But how are we to acquire prayer in this deep sense, prayer of simple gazing, prayer in which there is a personal encounter between us and God? How shall we begin?

Approaching Christ, teacher of prayer

In answer to the appeal of his disciples, "Teach us to pray", Christ gave them the Lord's Prayer; and this is indeed the model for all our praying. Yet, next to the Lord's Prayer used by Christians everywhere, there is a further way of praying that is particularly commended within the Orthodox Church to all who seek living, inner prayer; and that is the Jesus Prayer. This is a short invocation, frequently repeated, most commonly in the form "Lord Jesus Christ, Son of God, have mercy on me." "The brethren of Egypt", said St Augustine concerning the early monks, "offer frequent prayers that are very brief and suddenly shot forth."

The Jesus Prayer is precisely such an 'arrow prayer'. Another 'arrow prayer', used, for example, in the movement of Fr John Main, is the phrase *Maranatha*, "Our Lord, come" (*1 Co* 16:22). The Jesus Prayer differs from this in being centred specifically on the Holy Name 'Jesus', and therein lies its distinctive value. Used faithfully, as a regular part of our life in Christ, the Jesus Prayer can indeed bring us to the sense of the Divine Presence of which the old man spoke: "I just sit and look at God…"

The Four 'Strands'

"Lord Jesus Christ, Son of God, have mercy on me." The Jesus Prayer is brief and concise - ten words in English, only seven in Greek or Russian - yet at the same time it is remarkably complete. Within this one short sentence we may find combined four 'strands' or constituent elements:

1. the cry for mercy;
2. the discipline of repetition;
3. the quest for stillness (*hesychia*[1]);
4. the veneration of the Holy Name.

What is the origin of these four elements, and how did they come together to form the Jesus Prayer?

(1) The *cry for mercy*, "Lord, have mercy", *Kyrie eleison*, is found in liturgical worship from at least the 4th century, and its use in Christian prayer may well be more ancient. It is important in this context not to misinterpret the word *eleos*, 'mercy'. To ask for divine mercy is not to be seen as something gloomy and exclusively penitential. While the cry for mercy certainly involves sorrow for sin, it speaks also of divine forgiveness. It affirms that God's loving kindness and compassion are greater than my brokenness and guilt. Sometimes the Greek Fathers connect the word

eleos, 'mercy', with *elaion*, meaning 'olive oil'. This is probably bad etymology, but it is good theology. 'Mercy' signifies precisely the love of God, poured out to heal and restore.

The Jesus Prayer, then, with its appeal for mercy, is not to be seen as dark and sombre. It is, on the contrary, a prayer full of light and hope. St Hesychius of Sinai (? 8th century) summed up its true spirit by saying, "If we unceasingly call upon Jesus with a keen yearning that is full of sweetness and joy, then the air of our heart is filled with rejoicing and peace."

(2) The *discipline of repetition* is first found in an explicit form among the Desert Fathers of Egypt in the 4th century. Their daily work was of a very simple kind, such as basket-making and the plaiting of rush mats. How was a monk to occupy his mind, as he undertook such uniform and monotonous tasks? How could he fulfil St Paul's injunction, "Pray without ceasing" (*1 Th* 5:17)? The solution adopted by the Desert Fathers was to practise *monologia* or 'monologic prayer', that is, the repetition of a single word or phrase. They found that this discipline of repetition helps to simplify the mind, bringing it from fragmentation to unity.

The phrases repeated by the ascetics of Egypt were often a verse from Scripture, and especially from the Psalms, such as Psalm 50 [51]:1, "Have mercy upon me, O

God, according to Your great mercy", or Psalm 69 [70]:1, "O God, come to my aid; O Lord, make haste to help me." Non-Scriptural phrases could also be used. Abba Apollo sought to expiate a heavy sin of his youth by repeating, "As man, I have sinned; as God, do You forgive." The *Spiritual Homilies* attributed to St Macarius (? late 4th century) - Syrian rather than Egyptian in origin - suggest the prayer "I beseech You, I beseech You, O Lord." Other 'monologic prayers' used by Christians today, although not found among the Desert Fathers, include such phrases as "Lord, remember me in Your kingdom" (see the prayer of the Good Thief, *Lk* 23:42), and "Glory to You, O God, glory to You" (an invocation occurring at the start of most Orthodox services).

Saying the Holy Name

In the 4th-century Desert, then, there existed a variety of short prayers suitable for frequent repetition. Some of the 'monologic prayers' adopted by the early monks contained the name of Jesus: "Jesus, help me", "Lord Jesus, protect me from my tongue." But in the 4th century such formulae including the Holy Name enjoy no especial predominance, and so it is not as yet possible to speak of a specifically 'Jesus-centred' spirituality. That comes only in the 5th century and subsequently. In this way, the Jesus Prayer emerged initially as one among many such 'monologic' formulae. What led it to prevail as by far the most popular of the various formulae - although it has never possessed an exclusive monopoly - was the presence within it of the Holy Name of Jesus. (Of this we shall speak further when we come to the fourth 'strand'.) As the Desert Fathers recognised, and as contemporary psychologists confirm, the discipline of repetition is an intense and powerful method of recollection. It needs to be used with discretion.

(3) The *quest for stillness* (*hesychia*), the third of our four strands, also emerged among the monks of 4th-century Egypt. "When you pray," wrote one of their leading spokesmen, Evagrius of Pontus (346-99), "do not shape within yourself any image of the Deity, and do not let your intellect be stamped with the impress of any form… Prayer is a putting-away of thoughts." He did not, of course, intend this as a description of all forms of prayer, for liturgical worship certainly involves a multiplicity of images and symbols. He was concerned simply to recommend, alongside liturgical worship and the study of Scripture, a particular type of prayer that may be called 'non-iconic'. Similar teaching about the renunciation of images and thoughts can be found in many Western texts, such as *The Cloud of Unknowing* (14th century), and *The Dark Night of the Soul* by St John of the Cross (16th century).

Evagrius did not suggest any practical method for attaining 'non-iconic' prayer. In the 5th century, however, St Diadochus of Photike proposed the 'remembrance' or invocation of Jesus as precisely a way of entry into the prayer of inner stillness:

> The intellect requires of us imperatively some task that will satisfy its need for activity. For the complete fulfilment of its purpose we should give it nothing but the prayer *Lord Jesus*... Let the intellect continually concentrate on these words within its inner shrine with such intensity that it is not turned aside to any mental images.

In this way, Diadochus linked together two of our four 'strands': the discipline of repetition and the quest for *hesychia*. Repetition will assist us in stilling our ever-active mind, and so will enable us to acquire prayer of interior silence.

The doorway to 'non-iconic' prayer

Subsequent writers in the Orthodox spiritual tradition consistently follow Diadochus in regarding the Jesus Prayer as a doorway into 'non-iconic' prayer. This means that the Jesus Prayer is not a form of meditation on specific incidents in the life of Christ. It is in this way different from the methods of discursive meditation commended in the Catholic West since the era of the Counter-Reformation by, for example, St Ignatius Loyola or St Francis de Sales. In such meditation a person makes full use of the imagination, picturing a scene from the Gospels, visualising himself as one of those present, seeing in his mind's eye Jesus approaching him and speaking to him; and then with his faculty of will he makes specific resolutions. While there is certainly nothing wrong with such discursive meditation, the Jesus Prayer adopts a different path. When using the Prayer, we seek to still our imagination. Instead of calling to mind incidents from the life of Christ, we dwell upon his total and immediate presence. When visual images occur, we set them aside. We do not engage in chains of reasoning or a string of resolutions. We think solely of Jesus himself.

A more positive approach

Many people are bewildered by this requirement to lay aside images and thoughts. They try to do this but find that it lies beyond their power. In such a situation it is wise to adopt an approach that is positive rather than negative. Instead of emphasising what we want to get rid of, let us rather concentrate on what we hope to acquire. Instead of saying to ourselves, "Drive out all distracting thoughts", let us say rather, "Think with loving tenderness of the Saviour Jesus." What we are seeking is not so much a mind stripped of images as a heart full of love. Images and thoughts will constantly rise up within us. Let them recede into the background. In the foreground, put Jesus.

(4) The *veneration of the Holy Name* is without doubt the most decisive and significant of the four 'strands'. The

theology of the Divine Name has distant roots. The Old Testament displays a profound reverence for the name of God: in the words of the prophet Malachi (1:11), "From the rising of the sun to its setting My name is great among the nations." So strong was the awe inspired by God's name that the Tetragrammaton - the four consonants comprising the name 'Yahweh', 'Lord' - was usually not pronounced aloud in later Judaism.

This Jewish exaltation of the Holy Name continued in the New Testament. In the prayer to God the Father that Christ entrusted to his disciples, he included the clause "Hallowed be Thy name". At the Last Supper he went further, teaching them to pray not only in the name of the Father but likewise in his own name (*Jn* 16:23-24). St Peter, in his confession of faith before the Sanhedrin immediately after Pentecost, spoke of the healing virtue possessed by "the name of Jesus Christ of Nazareth", insisting that "there is no other name under heaven by which we must be saved" (*Ac* 4:10,12). Indeed, the literal meaning of the name 'Jesus' is precisely 'Saviour'; as the angel said to Joseph, "You shall call His name Jesus, for He will save His people from their sins" (*Mt* 1:21). When we use the Jesus Prayer, we are thus putting our trust in Jesus Christ as our personal Saviour. In the same spirit, St Paul regarded the name of Jesus as a focus of adoration: "At the name of Jesus every knee should bow" (*Ph* 2:10).

Heir to the Old and New Testament, the early Church reaffirmed this devotion to the Divine Name. In the words of Hermas, the 2nd-century author of *The Shepherd*, "The name of the Son of God is great and boundless, and it upholds the whole world." Diadochus of Photike, as we have seen, urged the constant repetition of the prayer *Lord Jesus*. "Sufficient for our defence against our enemies", wrote St Nilus of Ancyra (early 5th century), "is the name of Jesus Christ the most high God." "To rebuke the demons is possible only for the great ones who possess authority. … But all that is possible for us who are weak is to take refuge in the name of Jesus" said St John of Gaza (early 6th century). A similar love for the Holy Name was expressed in the medieval West, notably by St Bernard of Clairvaux (1090-1153). Paraphrasing Bernard, the Yorkshireman Richard Rolle, hermit of Hampole (d. 1349), exclaimed: "Ah! Ah! that wonderful name! Ah! that delectable name! This is the name that is above all names… Verily the name of Jesus is in my mind a joyous song, and heavenly music in mine ear, and in my mouth a honeyed sweetness."

The dynamic presence of Jesus

This belief in the intrinsic sanctity and numinous force of the Holy Name of Jesus is fundamental to the spirituality of the Jesus Prayer. We shall not even begin to appreciate the meaning of the Jesus Prayer unless we recognise how the name of Jesus is felt to contain within itself grace and power. There is an integral connection between the name and the one who is named. "A name", said Origen (d. around 254), "brings before us the distinctive character of what is named." To call upon a person by name is to render that person dynamically present, and this is especially true when we call by name upon Jesus. The Holy Name is endowed with sacramental force. It is an effective sign, an outward and visible token of an inner and spiritual grace.

A 'Jesus-centred' spirituality

Thus the key figure in the emergence of the Jesus Prayer, who binds together three out of the four constituent 'strands', is Diadochus of Photike in the 5th century. While devotion to the Holy Name is found before his time, he is the first to emphasise with some frequency the specific invocation of the Name in the prayer *Lord Jesus* (in the vocative). Nilus, his elder contemporary, also makes occasional references to the invocation of Jesus, but they are scattered and undeveloped. In Diadochus we find for the first time a 'Jesus-centred' spirituality. Whether he intended the phrase *Lord Jesus* to be followed by other words is possible, but he did not made this clear. At the same time, as we have already noted, he regarded the repetition ('strand' two) of this invocation to the Lord Jesus as a way of gathering together our dispersed attention, and so introducing it into unified stillness ('strand' three).

Diadochus did not place particular emphasis upon the first of our four 'strands', the cry for mercy. But this is prominent at the beginning of the next century in St John of Gaza and his companion St Barsanuphius. Combining the Bishop of Photike with the two Elders of Gaza, we have all the essential components of the Jesus Prayer. Later authors do no more than build upon the foundations that they have laid.

Find Christ Everywhere:
Ways of Practising the Jesus Prayer

The Jesus Prayer may be practised in two ways. There is first what may be called the 'free' use, when it is said once or many times as we go about our familiar occupations, during all the passing moments of the day that might otherwise be wasted. Then there is the 'fixed' use, when we repeat the Jesus Prayer as part of our appointed times for prayer, when our whole attention is concentrated on the act of praying. We can choose to follow the 'free' use without necessarily adopting the 'fixed' use as well.

The purpose of the 'free' use can be summed up in the words 'Find Christ everywhere'. The aim of the 'fixed' use can best be expressed in the phrase 'Create silence'.

Let us explore these two forms of the Jesus Prayer. The Prayer in its 'free' use may be practised at any time and in any place. We can repeat it in our room, while at work, as we walk about in the street. We can say it at the bus stop, in our car when stopped by the red light, in church when we arrive before the beginning of the service. It can be our first thought as we wake in the morning, and our last thought before we go to sleep at night. I find it helpful at committee meetings! It can be easily taught to children.

Because it is a short and simple prayer, instantly available without any special preparation, the Jesus Prayer can be used in situations where a more complex form of prayer would be impossible. We can repeat it when unable to sleep, when subject to physical pain or mental distress, or at moments of temptation and sudden crisis. It is a prayer for all seasons, especially suitable for our contemporary age of anxiety, living as we do in a time-starved society. The Jesus Prayer is never out of place.

Making the secular sacred

The effect, then, of the 'free use' of the Jesus Prayer is to integrate our prayer time and our work time, to turn our work itself into prayer, and so to make the secular sacred. In the words of a Russian spiritual master of the 19th century, St Theophan the Recluse (1815-94), "The hands at work, the mind and heart with God." "A Christian", said the Russian-American Fr Alexander Schmemann (1921-83), "is the one who, wherever he or she looks, finds everywhere Christ, and rejoices in Him."

That is exactly what the Jesus Prayer helps us to do. Through our invocation of the Holy Name, all persons and all things around us become transparent. We begin to see all things in Christ, and Christ in all things. In one of the *agrapha* or 'unwritten sayings' - words of Jesus that circulated among the early Christians but are not included in the New Testament - it is said: "Lift the stone, and you

will find Me; cut the wood in two, and there am I." Such is
the result of the 'free' use.

If, however, we are to bring prayer into each passing
moment, into every familiar occupation, then we need
a form of praying that is immediately at hand, directly
accessible without elaborate reflection. The Jesus Prayer is
precisely such a form of praying. When recited regularly in
a 'free' way, it comes to our mind and lips spontaneously,
without any deliberate effort on our part. To use Theophan's
term, it becomes "self-acting". So it gradually pervades
every part of our daily life, enabling each activity and each
personal encounter to be Spirit-filled.

Bridging the gap

Becoming "self-acting" in this way, the Jesus Prayer
reaches out from our consciousness into the unconscious.
Even when we are not reciting the Prayer, yet at a
profound level of our being an awareness of God's love
has not ceased to be present within us, like an afterglow
following the sunset. The Jesus Prayer can sometimes
flow over into our sleep. In *The Way of the Pilgrim*, the
anonymous Russian wanderer of the title, who recited
the Prayer continually, recorded that one morning "the
Prayer woke me up". Before he was fully awake, he
found that he was already repeating the Prayer. Others
have experienced something similar during an operation
under total anaesthetic. They have been reciting the Jesus

Prayer before lapsing into unconsciousness; and then, on regaining consciousness several hours later, the first thing of which they become aware is that they are saying the Prayer.

While the 'free' use of the Jesus Prayer can be practised during empty moments or when carrying out routine tasks, it is less appropriate when we are engaged in some absorbing activity that requires full concentration. When I am counselling others or when as priest I am hearing confessions, before we begin or during pauses I will silently invoke the name of Jesus on the person before me; but while the other is actually speaking, I try to listen with the whole of my attention. It is unwise to attempt to do two things at once, for then in all probability we shall do both things badly. St James in his Epistle warned us not to be *dipsychos*, 'double-minded' or 'divided in our psyche' (*Jm* 1:8). A surgeon, performing a delicate operation in which the slightest mistake might prove fatal, would scarcely be well-advised to keep breaking off from the task at hand in order to say prayers. But he might certainly wish to say the Jesus Prayer before embarking on the operation and after it is finished.

Establishing a sense of God's presence

"Pray without ceasing" said St Paul (*1 Th* 5:17). Some Christian groups, such as the 4th-century Messalians, interpreted this to mean that we are to *say prayers* all the time. But this is not literally possible, for we have sometimes to eat, brush our teeth or gargle. Prayer, however, understood in a more extended sense, is not limited to the enunciation of words, but it signifies what St Gregory of Nyssa (330-?395) termed a 'sense of presence'. The aim of the Jesus Prayer is to establish within us this 'sense of presence', which will continue to exist at a deep level of our being even after we have stopped repeating the actual words of the Prayer.

That surely is what St Paul meant by unceasing prayer: an implicit state rather than a series of explicit acts. Yet, in order that this implicit state may genuinely exist within us, it requires to be sustained by outward prayers, frequently repeated. In this way, the regular use of the Jesus Prayer initiates us into the first beginnings of continual prayer.

Create Silence

What, in the second place, is the function of the 'fixed' use of the Jesus Prayer?

"If I were a doctor," said the Danish philosopher Søren Kierkegaard, "and were asked for my advice, I would say: Create silence!" Assailed by mobile phones and piped music, we are sorely in need of such a doctor. Silence - "the universal language", as Fr Lawrence Freeman has described it - is one of the primary sources of our personhood, and without it we are not authentically human. In the words of Friedrich von Hügel, "Man is what he does with his silence."

The nature of spiritual silence

Yet what do we mean by silence? Is it merely negative - an absence of sound, a pause between words? Surely not. In its deeper spiritual sense, silence is not negative but positive, not an emptiness or void but a fullness. "Silence is a presence," said Georges Bernanos, "at the heart of it is God." We are told in the Psalms, "Be still and know that I am God" (*Ps* 45[46]:10). The Psalmist does not merely enjoin us to refrain from speech - "Be still" - but in positive terms he urges us to be aware of the Divine: "Know that

I am God." Silence in the religious sense signifies God-awareness. What matters in silence is not our external situation but our inner disposition. It is a matter, not of keeping our mouth shut, but of opening our heart to God.

Silence, then, properly understood, implies not isolation but relationship. It denotes, in the context of worship, not rejection of the Other but acceptance. It is an attitude of receptivity and, above all, of *listening*. Like the child Samuel in the temple, the one who seeks silence is appealing to God: "Speak, Lord, for Your servant hears" (*1 S* 3:9-10). Silence implies 'being with', in an alert manner: a losing and finding of oneself in the Other.

The key to prayer: listening

In the Roman catacombs there is to be seen, painted on the wall, the figure of a woman with uplifted hands, gazing up to heaven in prayer. Who is she? The Virgin Mary, a figure of the Church, or the human soul at worship? Or all three things at once? Whatever the answer, this depiction of the *Orans* expresses exactly what it means to be silent. The one who is silent - the hesychast, to use the Orthodox term - is *par excellence* the one who listens, who waits expectantly upon the Spirit.

Yet, when we pray, how can we manage to stop talking and to start listening? That is the crucial difficulty encountered by all who seek to acquire inner prayer; and it is here that the Jesus Prayer can help us. All too often, when we attempt to be still, we are assailed by a stream of distracting thoughts, like buzzing flies or mosquitoes on a summer evening. The thoughts are not necessarily impure or evil, but they are aimless and futile, irrelevant to the work of prayer. What are we to do? It is of little use to say to ourselves "Stop thinking." We are unable to turn off the internal television set by a simple act of will. The human mind cannot rest idle. The solution is to satisfy our ever-active mind by assigning to it a simple and unifying task: the repeated invocation of the Holy Name of Jesus. "You must bind the mind", said Theophan the Recluse, "with one thought, or the thought of the One only."

The Jesus Prayer is a prayer in words. Yet it is also a prayer of listening, a contemplative prayer that enables us to wait on the Spirit. When we invoke the Holy Name, our attitude is that of the *Orans* with her hands raised to heaven. Because the words of the Prayer are few and straightforward, and because they are regularly repeated, it is a prayer that leads us through words into silence; or, more exactly, that enables us to discover the silence hidden at the heart of the words.

Dwelling in God's presence

Sometimes, when saying the Jesus Prayer, we will be moved to stop repeating the words and merely to dwell in God's presence, quiet and recollected. Our best moments of prayer often take that form. On such occasions, then, let us suspend the Prayer for a time, until we find that our mind is wandering astray; and then we can once more resume the invocation "Lord Jesus…". In general, however, it is important to persist with a concerted effort in the actual recitation of the words of the Jesus Prayer. St John Climacus, the 7th-century abbot of Mount Sinai, rightly insisted, "Contain your mind *within the words of prayer*." As Fr John Main has warned us, we do not want to float off into a "holy-dozy" state in which we are not really praying at all, but are merely half-asleep.

Of course, unless we are great saints, we will constantly suffer from distracting thoughts. There is no reason to be surprised at that. What we have to do, every time our thoughts have wandered, is to bring them back to the work of prayer. This we must do again and again, without being discouraged. As St Romuald of Camaldoli (d. 1027) wrote, "If your mind wanders, do not give up; hurry back and apply your mind to the words once more." Herein exactly lies the special value of the Jesus Prayer. When our attention has drifted away, we do not have to ask ourselves, "Where was I? What was I going to say next?" For the Jesus Prayer is immediately close at hand, and we have only to take up once more the regular invocation of the Holy Name.

A Small Murmuring Stream

There is liberty and flexibility in the invocation of the Name. The exact words may vary. The usual form, "Lord Jesus Christ, Son of God, have mercy on me", is based on the prayer of the blind beggar Bartimaeus outside Jericho: "Jesus, Son of David, have mercy on me" (*Lk* 18:38; *Mk* 10:47). Frequently the words "a sinner" are added at the end: "...have mercy on me a sinner". This recalls the prayer of the tax collector (the publican) in the temple, "God be merciful to me a sinner" (*Lk* 18:13), and it gives to the Jesus Prayer a more penitential character.

These are not the only possibilities. Some Orthodox prefer to use the plural, "...have mercy on us", thereby including others in an explicit way. We may even say "...have mercy on us and on the world". We can say "...Son of the living God" (see *Mt* 16:16). We can introduce the communion of saints, saying "Lord Jesus Christ, at the prayers of the Mother of God, have mercy on me", or else, "...at the prayers of St N. ..." (mentioning our patron saint), or "...through the protection of my guardian angel...". We are all of us at liberty to choose the form of words that suits us best. But we do well not to change our chosen form of words too often. Shrubs that are frequently transplanted do not put down roots!

Those who have advanced somewhat in the practice of the Jesus Prayer may find the standard formula too long, and so they may abbreviate it: "Lord Jesus, have mercy", "My Jesus", or even the Holy Name 'Jesus' on its own. This last, however, is uncommon in the Christian East; the name 'Jesus' repeated by itself is felt to be almost too powerful and condensed, so that we prefer to 'dilute' it with other words. In the West, on the other hand - and not least in the English Middle Ages - the invocation 'Jesus' on its own has been widespread.

Underlying all these variations of formula, there is one element which remains unchanged; and that is the inclusion of the specific name 'Jesus'. The designation 'Jesus Prayer' can thus be applied in principle to *any* short prayer that contains the Holy Name.

Allowing God to act

At what speed should the Jesus Prayer be recited? Here again there is freedom. On the whole, the words are said more quickly in the Greek practice and more slowly in the Russian. In my own experience, I find that it takes about a quarter of an hour or twenty minutes to recite the Prayer a hundred times, but I know that others take longer than this. It is advisable to leave a short pause - less than a second - at the end of each Prayer, to prevent us from lapsing into overdrive and forgetting what it is that we are saying. The words of the Jesus Prayer may be recited aloud, and this is particularly helpful for those who are first beginning to use the Prayer. Alternatively, they may be articulated inwardly; but it is not usual in Orthodox practice for them to be chanted.

For how long at a time should the Jesus Prayer be recited? Once more, there is no unvarying rule. Some feel called to make the Jesus Prayer the centre of their whole spiritual life, perhaps repeating it for more than an hour each morning and each evening. Some, on the other hand, use texts from the liturgical books alongside the Jesus Prayer during their appointed times for prayer. Others again employ the Jesus Prayer only in a 'free' way. For those first beginning the 'fixed' use, it is enough to say the Prayer for no more than ten or fifteen minutes. Later on, the length of time may be increased.

Reciting the Jesus Prayer

The Jesus Prayer should never be said in an obsessive and insistent manner, as if we were seeking to impose our own will on that of God. The symbol of true prayer is not the clenched fist but the opened hands. When we pray, let us not try to coerce God, but let us merely place ourselves at his disposition and let us allow him to act. The words of the Jesus Prayer are not to be recited with exaggerated emphasis, but they should flow "like a small murmuring stream", to quote Starets Partheny of Kiev (1790-1855).[2] The point has been well made by the French Orthodox monk-priest Lev Gillet (1893-1980), in his classic work *On the Invocation of the Name of Jesus*:

> A common mistake of beginners is to wish to associate the invocation of the Holy Name with inner intensity or emotion. They try to say it with great force. But the Name of Jesus is not to be shouted, or fashioned with violence, even inwardly. When Elijah was commanded to stand before the Lord, there was a great and strong wind, but the Lord was not in the wind; and after the wind an earthquake, but the Lord was not in the earthquake; and after the earthquake a fire, but the Lord was not in the fire. And after the fire came a still small voice: "And it was so, when Elijah heard it, that he wrapped his face in his mantle, and went out, and stood…" (*1 K* 19:13).

Although artificial emotion is inappropriate, there are occasions during the saying of the Jesus Prayer when a person may be moved to tears. As with prayer in general, so with tears in particular: we are not to use force. The tears should flow naturally, quietly and calmly, without violent sobbing or contortions of the face. When such tears arise spontaneously, they may be accepted as a gift and an added blessing.

It is normal, when following the 'fixed' use, to be seated while reciting the Jesus Prayer. In Orthodox monastic practice, the hesychast often sits on a low stool, about ten inches high, in a crouching position. This will quickly become uncomfortable. It is better, when first embarking on the Prayer, to sit with a straight spine on an upright chair with a back (preferably not an easy chair). The legs should not be crossed while praying. In some stricter monasteries the Prayer is said standing, accompanied by prostrations to the ground, but this is not usual among lay persons.

The Jesus Prayer is commonly recited with the eyes closed. Most frequently it is said alone, as Christ enjoins: "… in your room, with the door shut… in secret" (*Mt* 6:6). Monks and nuns say it, each in their own cell, especially in the late evening after Compline or before the morning Office. But sometimes it is also said communally, for example in the Orthodox Monastery of St John the Baptist at Tolleshunt Knights (Essex), founded by Fr Sophrony (Sakharov) (1896-1993). Here, when the members assemble in church, they do not say the Prayer aloud all together, which might prove noisy and restless. First one person recites it, perhaps a hundred times, and then another takes up the invocation, each singly in turn, while the others repeat the Prayer inwardly. Visitors to the monastery can testify that this produces an effect of profound stillness and concentration.

Praying in community

Several Orthodox parishes have taken up this communal use of the Jesus Prayer, following the practice at Tolleshunt

Knights. Parishioners meet in church perhaps once a week, for thirty minutes or an hour. This has proved pastorally very beneficial. Groups can also meet, saying the Jesus Prayer each inwardly but not aloud. Whether or not it is accompanied by the Jesus Prayer, shared silence has great dynamism. Those who attend Quaker meetings can testify to that.

One of the advantages of the Jesus Prayer is that it does not presuppose any special knowledge or detailed preparation. To those who wish to use it, we can say: *Simply begin.* Be at rest, and yet alert. In the words once more of Fr Lev: "Do not think that you are invoking the Name; think only of Jesus Himself. Say His Name slowly, softly and quietly."

Three Things to Help Us

There are three things that can assist us in the recitation of the Jesus Prayer. The first is more personal, the other two more external.

A 'soul friend'

It is, in the first place, highly desirable to find what in Celtic Christianity is called a 'soul friend' (*amchara*): a spiritual father or mother, an 'elder' (in Greek, *geronta*; in Russian, *starets*), who can advise us in the practice of the Prayer. Such a person need not necessarily be a priest. He or she may also be a lay monk or a nun, or someone in the 'world', man or woman. What is important is that the 'soul friend' should possess personal experience. If we are climbing a mountain for the first time, we do well to ascend with somebody who has been up before and who knows the way. So it is with the ascent of prayer.

And what are we to do if we cannot find a spiritual guide? Does that mean that we should not use the Jesus Prayer? Not at all. Even without guidance, there is no danger in adopting the Jesus Prayer, so long as we say it simply, humbly, and for limited periods. But it is much better to have a 'soul friend'. If we search, God will give us the support that we need.

The prayer rope

Secondly, and on a somewhat different level, we may be assisted in saying the Jesus Prayer by the employment of a prayer rope (in Greek, *komvoschoinion*; in Russian, *tchotki*). This is a circle or chaplet, usually made of wool or twine, with perhaps a hundred knots; but the number varies. One Jesus Prayer is said at each knot. It can also be made of leather, or it may consist of beads, in which case it somewhat resembles the Catholic rosary, except that it accompanies the invocation of Jesus, not the *Hail Mary*.

The Orthodox prayer rope should not be confused with the worry beads (*komvologion*) used by Greek men at times of relaxation. Possibly the *komvoschoinion* and the *komvologion* share a common origin, but in practice their function is different. I remember how a non-Orthodox friend of mine returned with great enthusiasm from his first visit to Greece. "It is a wonderful country!" he told me. "Even when the men are sitting in the cafés, smoking, drinking ouzo, playing cards, they are all reciting the Jesus Prayer." Unfortunately he had not appreciated the difference between the *komvoschoinion* and the *komvologion*!

While the prayer rope can be used to measure the number of times that we say the Jesus Prayer, this is not its only function. In any case, mere quantity is not of primary importance in the recitation of the Prayer. In the words of St Isaac the Syrian (7th century), "I do not want to count milestones, but to enter the bridal chamber." The main purpose of the prayer rope is not to act as a measurement but to assist us to concentrate. It is a fact of experience that if, when praying, we involve the body, giving our hands something to do, this will steady and centre us. The act of passing the knots of the prayer rope through our fingers will stop us fidgeting and will establish a regular rhythm in our invocation.

Praying with each breath

To reinforce our offering of the Jesus Prayer, there is thirdly a psychosomatic method, co-ordinating the rhythm of the Prayer with the tempo of our breathing. "Remember God more often than you breathe" said St Gregory of Nazianzus (329-90). If we synchronise the words of the Prayer with the movement of inhalation and exhalation, this will render the invocation more constant and continuous. The simplest way of doing this is to recite the first part of the Prayer, "Lord Jesus Christ, Son of God", as we breathe in, and the second part, "have mercy on me, a sinner", as we breathe out. At the same time, the speed of our breathing should be slowed down. There are other more intricate techniques for the control of the respiration, but these should be attempted only by those under the personal direction of an experienced guide. It is a delicate matter to interfere with our breathing.

Alongside the control of the respiration, some Orthodox also employ a form of 'inner exploration', whereby the attention is concentrated upon particular psychosomatic centres. We picture the mind or intellect passing, with our breath, down through our lungs into the heart. Once more we are advised not to attempt such techniques unless we have proper guidance.

Between the Orthodox psychosomatic methods and the physical techniques found in Hindu Yoga and among the Sufis of Islam, there are interesting parallels. It is probable that the Byzantine hesychasts were influenced by these non-Christian practices, although it is not clear precisely when and how this influence occurred. At the same time, we should not overlook the distinctively Christian character of the Jesus Prayer. It is not simply a rhythmic mantra, designed to enhance concentration, but a personal invocation addressed specifically to the second person of the Trinity, Jesus Christ, that is, to the one who was born in Bethlehem, who died on the cross and rose from the dead, and whose second coming we await. What matters is not just *how* we pray but *to whom*.

Faith and love

In any case, the breathing techniques and the methods of inner exploration are no more than external aids, useful to some but in no way obligatory upon all. They do not constitute the essence of the Jesus Prayer. For the true and full practice of the invocation of the Name, no other technique is needed except a living faith in Jesus Christ as

Son of God and Saviour, and an active love for his ever-present Person.

These two things, faith and love, are indeed indispensable. There is sacramental grace present in the Holy Name, but the Jesus Prayer is not a magic talisman. "A mere repetition of the words does not signify anything" said Theophan the Recluse. Christ warned us against the use of "vain repetitions" in prayer, against the heaping up of empty phrases (*Mt* 6:7). But the Jesus Prayer is not a "vain repetition", if it is recited, as it should be, with fear of God, and with faith and love.

Prayer of the Heart

It is customary in Orthodoxy, as in Western Christianity, to distinguish three levels of prayer: of the lips, of the mind, and of the heart. This threefold distinction applies in particular to the Jesus Prayer.

(1) To begin with, the Jesus Prayer, like any other, is a prayer of the lips, an oral prayer.

(2) Yet prayer said *only* with the lips is obviously not true prayer. The mind, with its power of attention, needs also to be involved. We may recall the admonition of John Climacus: "Contain your *mind* within the words of prayer." So the Jesus Prayer grows gradually more inward. Yet we are not to be too quick in giving up the actual recitation of the words, whether spoken aloud or formed silently within us.

(3) Finally, by the grace of God, the mind is united with the heart, so that our prayer becomes 'prayer of the heart' or, more exactly, 'prayer of the mind in the heart".

By 'heart', in this context, Orthodox writers do not mean primarily the emotions and feelings, but the spiritual centre of the total human being. The heart, as well as being a physical organ in our chest, represents symbolically the focal point of our personhood as created in the image and likeness of God. The heart is thus the ground of our being, the root and source of our inner truth. It includes the emotions, but more significantly it comprises our will, our reason, and also the higher visionary faculty known in Greek as the *nous*, whereby we apprehend the glory of God. In the words of Theophan the Recluse, "The heart is the innermost self, or spirit. Here are located self-awareness, the conscience, the idea of God and of one's complete dependence on Him, and all the eternal treasures of the spiritual life."

As well as being the centre of our created personhood, the heart is also the point of encounter between each created person and the uncreated God. It is the gateway to self-transcendence, the place of divine indwelling. "Within the heart are unfathomable depths" it is stated in the *Spiritual Homilies* attributed to St Macarius. "…The heart is Christ's palace: there Christ the King comes to take His rest, with the angels and the spirits of the saints, and He dwells there, walking within it and placing His Kingdom there."

'Prayer of the heart', therefore, in Orthodox writings means not just 'affective prayer' in the Western sense but prayer of the entire human person, prayer in which body, soul and spirit are all participating. Moreover, since the heart is the meeting-place with God, prayer of the heart denotes not simply *my prayer* but *the prayer of Christ in me*. In St Paul's words, "It is no longer I who live, but Christ lives in me" (*Ga* 2:20).

The light of the Transfiguration

According to the mystical theology of the Orthodox Church, the faithful practice of the Jesus Prayer may lead, if God so wills, to a vision of light. This light that is beheld during prayer is not a physical and created light, but spiritual and uncreated. It is identical with the light that was seen by the three disciples at Christ's Transfiguration on Mount Tabor. St Gregory Palamas (1296-1359) taught that this divine light is nothing less than the eternal energies of God; but he made a careful distinction between the essence of God and his energies. The saints participate in the divine energies, but not in the divine essence, which remains always beyond participation. St Thomas Aquinas upheld the same teaching, in somewhat different terms, when he argued that there can be no *total* comprehension of the divine essence, even in the age to come.

Sometimes this uncreated light is manifested outwardly in the body of the hesychast. The great Russian *starets* of the 19th century, St Seraphim of Sarov (1754-1833), was seen transfigured with light by his follower Nicolas Motovilov. As the latter recounted:

Imagine in the centre of the sun, in the dazzling light of its midday rays, the face of someone talking to you. You see the movement of his lips and the changing expression of his eyes, you hear his voice, you feel someone holding your shoulders; yet you do not see his hands, you do not see his body, but only a blinding light spreading far around.

Such revelations of divine light may seem far beyond our present experience and capacity. Yet it is vital for us to recognise that such things happen, in our own day as in the past. As Fyodor Dostoevsky remarked, the realist finds no difficulty in accepting the existence of miracles. We ourselves may have progressed only a short way upon the path of the Jesus Prayer, but it is a path that leads out of time into eternity, and out of space into infinity.

The Holy Trinity and the Jesus Prayer

The Jesus Prayer is an appeal addressed specifically to Jesus Christ. It speaks of his Godhead, calling him "Lord" and "Son of God". At the same time we address him by his earthly name "Jesus", the name given to him at his human birth in Bethlehem by his mother the Virgin Mary and his foster-father Joseph. Thus in the Jesus Prayer we confess our faith in the central truth of Christianity: that Jesus is fully and entirely God and at the same time fully and entirely human, one single person in two complete natures. The cross and resurrection are not explicitly mentioned in the Jesus Prayer, but they are, of course, implicit. We are calling upon the total Christ.

At the same time the Jesus Prayer is not only Christological but Trinitarian. By invoking Jesus as "Son of God", at once we think also of his Father. Furthermore, the Spirit is likewise present in the Prayer, although he is not named. One of the Scriptural texts quoted by almost every writer on the Jesus Prayer is 1 Corinthians 12:3, "No one can say 'Lord Jesus' except in the Holy Spirit." The Spirit, while remaining anonymous, is the embracing 'environment' of the invocation of the Name. Gerard Manley Hopkins compared the Holy Virgin to the air we breathe: "Be thou then, O thou dear / Mother, my atmosphere."

We can apply this to the Jesus Prayer: the Holy Spirit is the 'atmosphere' in which the Prayer is said. Reciting the Jesus Prayer, then, we are praying *in* the Spirit *to* Christ, and *through* Christ *to* the Father. All three persons in the Trinity are included. The Jesus Prayer draws us into the *perichoresis* of the Trinity, the interchange or unceasing movement of mutual love that passes between the Eternal Three.[3]

The pattern within the Prayer

There is within this Trinitarian Jesus Prayer a tidal wave, a pattern of ascent and return. We mount up towards God in adoration as we say the first part of the Prayer, "Lord Jesus Christ, Son of God…". Then we return to ourselves in grateful repentance, "…have mercy on me, a sinner." Thus the Jesus Prayer, more particularly in its expanded form ("…a sinner"), embraces the two primary 'moments' of Christian devotion: doxology, the 'moment' of gazing upwards towards God's glory; and compunction, the 'moment', both sorrowful and yet joyful, when we acknowledge that we are sinners who have been forgiven. As Bishop Simon Barrington-Ward has put it, "What matters is this holding together of rejoicing and yearning."

The Sacraments and the Jesus Prayer

"It is the sacraments that constitute our life in Christ" said St Nicolas Cabasilas (14th century). How, then, does the 'way of the Name' relate to the mysteries of Baptism and the Eucharist?

One of the great hesychast teachers, St Gregory of Sinai (d. 1346), described prayer as "Baptism made manifest". Developing the point with reference to the Jesus Prayer, he explained that in Baptism we receive the indwelling presence of Christ and the Spirit. It is not possible to imagine any gift greater than this, nor can anything be added to it. Baptismal grace is complete and perfect. Initially, however, receiving Baptism in infancy (as most of us do), we are unconscious of this indwelling presence. The whole purpose of the Christian life is precisely to experience actively this baptismal gift that has been already conferred upon us; to advance, that is, from grace present within us secretly and unconsciously, to grace at work within us "with full assurance and conscious awareness", as Gregory put it. In our beginning is our end; we are to *become what we are*.

There are two chief ways, said Gregory, in which this can be brought to pass: through "the fulfilment of the commandments", that is, through moral effort; and through "the methodical and unceasing invocation of the Lord Jesus". He added: "The first way is slower and the second shorter." Probably Gregory should not be interpreted as implying that these two ways are alternatives; for obviously everyone is required to "fulfil the commandments" and to observe moral rules. Equally, in calling the way of the Jesus Prayer "shorter" he cannot have meant that it is a 'soft option'; for in fact he made it abundantly clear that it involves firm commitment and persistence. His meaning surely is that outward moral effort, if unaccompanied by inner prayer, turns the Christian life into a heavy burden, into a matter of obligation and duty. Inner prayer 'shortens' the journey in the sense that it gives to our spiritual struggle both depth and meaning, both a sense of direction and a spirit of joy.

Being Christ-bearers

The purpose of the Jesus Prayer, then, is to help us to discover directly and vividly how, by virtue of Baptism, we are Christ-bearers, sharing in his death and resurrection, and at the same time Spirit-bearers, aflame with the fire of Pentecost.

What Gregory said about the Jesus Prayer as a revelation of baptismal grace he applied also to the Eucharist. Through the Jesus Prayer we perform an 'inner liturgy', whereby we "offer up the Lamb of God upon the altar of the soul and partake of Him in communion". The Jesus Prayer 'internalises' the Eucharist. But this 'spiritual communion' cannot exist unless we are also partaking outwardly in the sacrament.

Another text that sets the Jesus Prayer firmly in a sacramental context is *Directions to Hesychasts* by St Kallistos and St Ignatios Xanthopoulos (late 14th century). This provides a synoptic view of the Jesus Prayer. It is a concise manual on its practical use that can be warmly recommended to all who seek to follow 'the way of the Name'. The two Xanthopouloi begin by speaking about Baptism. Following the teaching of Gregory of Sinai, they state that our aim in prayer and ascetic life is to return "to that perfect spiritual re-creation and renewal by grace that was given to us freely from on high at the beginning in the sacred font". Then, after giving detailed instructions about the practice of the Jesus Prayer, they end by discussing Holy Communion. This, they say, is to be "continual", and if possible daily. To receive the sacrament daily is in fact highly unusual in the Orthodox Church. Thus, in the work of the Xanthopouloi, the Jesus Prayer is 'sandwiched' between the primary Christian mysteries of Baptism and Eucharist.

Enriching the sacramental life

From the writings of the Sinaite and the Xanthopouloi, it is evident that the Jesus Prayer enriches the sacramental life but does not replace it. The invocation of the Name exists, not in isolation, but in an ecclesial and mysterial context. It presupposes membership of the Church and participation in the Church's sacraments.

What, then, are we to say about those 'spiritual seekers' in our own day - and there are many of them - who practise the Jesus Prayer without belonging to any church community? Perhaps they do not have any definite faith in Jesus Christ as Saviour. Are we to forbid them to use the Prayer? Surely not; for the Jesus Prayer is not our private possession. It has to be said, however, that such persons are in an irregular situation. Let us hope that the Jesus Prayer, through the grace present within it, will draw them gradually into active church membership.

Intercession and the Jesus Prayer

Prayer may be secret, but it is never solitary. We cannot pray truly for ourselves unless, at least implicitly, we are also praying for others as well. There is in the strict sense no such thing as 'private' prayer, for we are always praying in and with the community of the total Church. The Jesus Prayer is thus not only personal but corporate. Even when we are saying to Jesus, "…have mercy on *me*", we are tacitly including in our prayer all those on whose behalf Jesus died and rose again. This is made much clearer when we use the form "…have mercy on *us*".

A powerful form of intercession

Can we, however, use the Jesus Prayer in a more direct way as a prayer of intercession? May we say, "…have mercy on John…have mercy on Mary", mentioning by name those whom we have upon our heart? I know of people who use the Jesus Prayer in this way, and in itself there is nothing wrong about such a practice. But obviously it makes the Jesus Prayer into something different from what writers of the hesychast tradition had in view when they spoke of the Jesus Prayer as a 'putting away of thoughts', as a way of entry into inner stillness. My own practice is to intercede for others before I begin to say the Jesus Prayer, and sometimes afterwards as well. Yet, when I come to the recitation of the Prayer itself, I do not mention anyone by name, but turn solely to the Lord Jesus. I have not thereby rejected those for whom I need to pray; even though I do not mention them by name, they are still present in my heart as I invoke Jesus, whose love enfolds them all. But I do not choose, at that precise moment, to mention them explicitly.

The "Monk of the Eastern Church", Fr Lev Gillet, practised the Jesus Prayer as a form of intercession in a particularly striking way. A small, vulnerable figure, poorly dressed, he used to wander through the streets of London during the night hours, invoking the name of Jesus upon all those whom he passed, upon the homeless, the beggars, upon everyone in distress and moral danger. "The name of Jesus", he wrote, "is a concrete and powerful means of transfiguring others into their most profound and divine reality. Let us reach out toward the men and women whom we pass in the street, the factory or the office... If we see Jesus in everyone, if we say 'Jesus' over everyone, we will go through the world with a new vision and a new gift in our own heart."

Act - Out of the Stillness

There is, finally, a misunderstanding that needs to be dispelled. If we pray alone, with our eyes closed, saying repeatedly "...have mercy on me", are we not being egotistic and self-centred? Are we not evading our social responsibility and turning our back on the suffering of a broken world? This, indeed, is an objection that may be made not only against the Jesus Prayer but against all forms of contemplative prayer.

An answer may be found in two aphorisms. The first is from St Seraphim of Sarov: "Acquire inner peace, and thousands around you will find salvation." The second is from the one-time Secretary-General of the United Nations, Dag Hammarskjöld, in his striking spiritual diary *Markings*: "Understand - through the stillness; act - out of the stillness; conquer - in the stillness."

The acquisition of inner peace

"Acquire inner peace": that is exactly the aim of the Jesus Prayer. Yet this is not selfish, for it makes us an instrument of peace to others. Because we have prayed the Jesus Prayer alone and in secret - it may be for no more than ten or fifteen minutes in every day - then, during all the other minutes and hours of the day, we shall be available to others, open to their concerns, loving and Christ-like, in a way that would otherwise be impossible. As Fr John Main has put it, the meditator becomes a mediator.

Again, it is precisely the purpose of the Jesus Prayer to help us to "understand - through the stillness", so that we can then "act - out of the stillness". If our words and actions do *not* come out of the stillness of prayer, they turn out to be superficial and impotent. But if they have their source in stillness, they can prove words and actions of fire and healing. We cannot truly change the world unless we have ourselves been changed by prayer.

The Jesus Prayer is in this way not only a contemplative prayer, but a prayer that combines contemplation and action. It is a prayer that makes our contemplation active, and our action contemplative.

Homecoming

The effect of the Jesus Prayer has been rightly described as homecoming. It enables us to return home, becoming our own true self, the person whom God calls us to be. Yet paradoxically in coming home we have not ceased to travel onwards, for our inner journey has no end; and by returning into ourselves we have been enabled to reach out to others as never before.

The Jesus Prayer began as a monastic prayer among the solitaries of the Desert. But, especially in our own day, it has become a prayer used more and more by lay people, in both the East and the West, by both Orthodox and non-Orthodox. It can even be said that it is today being practised by more people than ever it was in the past. It has become universal in its appeal.

Yet we should not claim concerning the Jesus Prayer, "It is the only way." Nor should we assert, "It is the best way." But this at least we may say: "It has helped many; it has helped me; perhaps it will also help you."

Endnotes

[1] *Hesychia*: the Greek word for quiet or stillness. From this comes the word 'hesychast', meaning one who pursues inner stillness through the Jesus Prayer or in some other way. 'Hesychasm' denotes the tradition of contemplative prayer developed in the Christian East from the 4th century onwards.

[2] *Starets* (Russian), *geron* or *geronta* (Greek): literally 'old man' or 'elder'. Someone experienced in the spiritual life, although not necessarily old in years, who acts as a guide to others. When applied to a woman the title becomes *staritsa* or *gerontissa*.

[3] *Perichoresis*: a Greek word meaning literally 'circular movement'. It is applied to the interaction of the two natures, divine and human, within the incarnate Christ, and also to the 'round dance' of mutual love between the three persons of the Trinity.

Further Reading

A Monk of the Eastern Church (Lev Gillet), *On the Invocation of the Name of Jesus* (London: Fellowship of St Alban and St Sergius, 2002). Has in view the invocation of the name 'Jesus' on its own, but applies also to the developed Jesus Prayer.

A Monk of the Eastern Church (Lev Gillet), *The Jesus Prayer*, revised edition by Ware, K. (Crestwood, NY: St Vladimir's Seminary Press, 1987). Discusses the background in the Old and New Testaments, and the later development of the Prayer. A very helpful overview.

Barrington-Ward, S., *The Jesus Prayer: A Way of Contemplation* (Boston, MA: Pauline Books & Media, 2007). A sympathetic treatment by an Anglican.

Brianchaninov, I., *On the Prayer of Jesus*, new edition with foreword by Ware, K. (Boston/London: New Seeds, 2006). By a 19th-century Russian; quotes extensively from earlier sources.

Chariton, I., *The Art of Prayer: An Orthodox Anthology*, introduction by Timothy [=Kallistos] Ware (London: Faber & Faber, 1966). Mainly from Russian 19th-century writers, especially Theophan the Recluse.

Coomaraswamy, R., *The Invocation of the Name of Jesus As Practiced in the Western Church* (Louisville, KY: Fons Vitae, 1999). Texts from the Latin West.

Hausherr, I., *The Name of Jesus*, Cistercian Studies Series 44 (Kalamazoo: Cistercian Publications, 1978). Scholarly and historical; needs updating.

Ware, K., *The Power of the Name: The Jesus Prayer in Orthodox Spirituality*, Fairacres Publication 44 (new edition, Oxford: SLG Press, 1986). An introductory account, for Western readers.

Ware, K., "The Beginnings of the Jesus Prayer", in Ward, B. and Waller, R. (eds.), *Joy of Heaven: Springs of Christian Spirituality* (London: SPCK, 2003), pp. 1-29. On the four 'strands' in the Jesus Prayer, and how they first emerged.

Ware, K., "Prayer in Evagrius of Pontus and the Macarian Homilies", in Waller, R. and Ward, B. (eds.), *An Introduction to Christian Spirituality* (London: SPCK, 1999), pp. 14-30. On the meaning of 'prayer of the heart'.

The Pilgrim's Tale, translated by T. Allan Smith, with introduction by Pentkovsky, A., The Classics of Western Spirituality 95 (New York/ Mahwah: Paulist Press, 1999). The 'travel notes' of an anonymous 19th-century Russian, whose life was centred on the Jesus Prayer. Also known as *The Way of the Pilgrim*.

The Philokalia: The Complete Text, compiled by St Nikodimos of the Holy Mountain and St Makarios of Corinth, translated by Palmer, G.E.H., Sherrard, P. and Ware, K., (4 vols., London/Boston: Faber & Faber, 1979-1995) (vol. 5 still to come). The classic collection of Orthodox ascetic and mystical writings. On the Jesus Prayer, see especially Hesychius and Diadochus (vol. 1), *A Discourse on Abba Philimon* (vol. 2), Symeon the New Theologian, Nikiphoros the Monk, Gregory of Sinai and Gregory Palamas (vol. 4).

Writings from the Philokalia on Prayer of the Heart, translated by Kadloubovsky, E. and Palmer, G.E.H., (London: Faber & Faber, 1951). Contains Kallistos and Ignatios Xanthopoulos, *Directions to Hesychasts* (pp. 164-270).

Contemplative Meditation

Fr Matthew ODC

A genuine Christian guide on how to meditate - and the many practical fruits. This is an excellently written, thoughtful guide on contemplative meditation - on how to do it, and on how important it is for a disciple of Christ to carry an attentive spirit in a practical way into daily life. Fr Matthew's famous little text has become a classic, and has helped countless numbers to secure a simple and straightforward marriage between everyday living and, as he puts it, focusing our will, our heart, on God our loving Father. Far from escapism, genuine Christian meditation equips the disciple to live in the truth, and without fear.

D514   ISBN 978 1 86082 047 2

The Eastern Churches

Fr Robin Gibbons

The Eastern Churches are a diverse group ranging from large Churches like the Russian and Greek Orthodox to smaller ones like the Ethiopian Orthodox and the Eastern-rite Catholic Churches. This booklet explores how historical differences came about, what the status of each Church is, and what characterises the spiritual life and worship of our Eastern brethren. Only by understanding and respecting each other's differences will the Church be reunited and "breathe with both lungs", east and west.

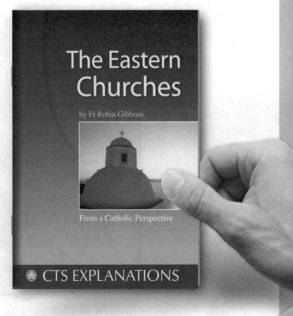

Ex19 ISBN 978 1 86082 357 2

Story of Prayer through Scripture

Fr Robert Taylerson

When Jesus taught his disciples and us to pray, he tapped into a story of prayer which stretched back to the book of Genesis and the very earliest recollections of humanity. This booklet follows the important Scriptural steps which led to the great tradition of Christian Prayer that we have today, including the great prayers of the Patriarchs and the Prophets, the Psalms in particular and those of Christ himself and the Apostolic writings of the New Testament.

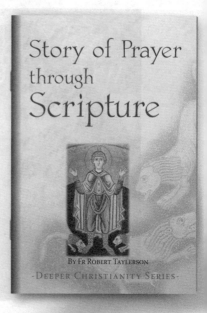

Story of Prayer
through
Scripture

By Fr Robert Taylerson

-Deeper Christianity Series-

SP26   ISBN 978 1 86082 523 1

Praying with Jesus

Pope Benedict XVI

Prayer was always an inner fountain which constantly flowed through the life, relationships, and actions of Jesus, guiding and strengthening him in his generous submission to God the Father's loving plan. Thus, Benedict XVI states that "Jesus is also the teacher of our prayer, indeed he is an active and fraternal support on every occasion in which we address the Father".

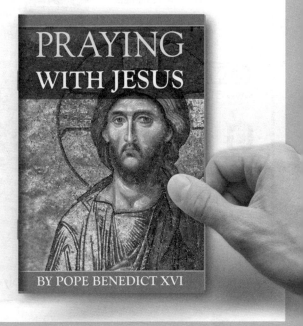

Do868   ISBN 978 1 86082 844 7